4/98

DATE DUE

WHAT·DO·WE·KNOW
ABOUT
BUDDHISM·?

ANITA GANERI

PETER BEDRICK BOOKS
NEW YORK

Published by
Peter Bedrick Books
2112 Broadway
New York, N.Y. 10023

© Macdonald Young Books 1997,
an imprint of Wayland Publishers Ltd.

Designer and illustrator: Celia Hart
Commissioning editor: Debbie Fox
Editor: Jayne Booth
Picture research: Jane Taylor
Consultant: Professor Peter Harvey

Library of Congress Cataloging-in-Publication Data
Ganeri, Anita. 1961-
    What do we know about Buddishm? / Anita Ganeri.
        p.   cm.
    Includes index
    Summary: Discusses the principles and practices of Buddishm,
    Including information about holy people and places, act, and
    festivals.
    ISBN 0-87226-389-4
    1. Buddishm--juvenile literature. [1. Buddishm] I. Title.
    BQ4032.G368   1997
294.3--dc21   96-52 161
                                                   CIP
                                                   AC

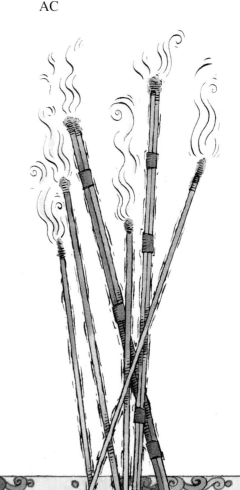

Photograph acknowledgements: Front and back cover:
Cephas; Bridgeman Art Library, p18 (The Mandala of
Sahasrabhuja Avalokitesvara, Tunhang, 9th century,
Indochinese, National Museum of India, New Delhi);
British Museum, p16; British Library, p33(b); Britstock,
p32 (Bernd Ducke); Cephas, p26(t) (Nigel Blythe); Clear
Vision, p22(r); Patrick G. Cockell, p9; James Davis
Travel Photography, pp8(b), 21(b), 25(b), 27; Eye
Ubiquitous pp21(tr), 23 (P. M. Field), 29(b) (John
Hulme), 35(l) David Cumming, 35(br) (Bennett Dean),
36(Tim Page); Robert Harding Picture Library, pp25(t),
28, 29(t), 31(b), 41(b) (Maurice Joseph); Michael
Holford, pp13(t), 15(t), 20; The Hutchison Library,
pp17(t) (Sarah Etherington), 19(l) (R. Ian Lloyd), 21(tl)
(Patricia Govcoolea), 37(b) (John Burbank); The Image
Bank, p8(t) (Guido A. Rossi); The Independent, p17(b);
Magnum Photos, p13(b) (Chris Steel-Perkins);
Bipinchandra J. Mistry, pp19(r), 22(l), 40; Zul Mukhida,
pp24, 37(t); Christine Osborne Pictures, pp15(b), 26(b);
Panos Pictures, pp30 (Cliff Venner), 31(t) & 38 (Jean-Léo
Dugart), 39(b) (Martin Flitman), 41(t) (Neil Cooper);
Bury Peerless, p12; Frank Spooner Pictures, pp33(t)
(Erik Sampers), 39(t); Spectrum Colour Library, p35(tr)
(W. R. Davis); Tantra Designs, endpapers (Peter Douglas)
& p14.

Printed in Hong Kong by Wing King Tong
00 99 98 97 1 2 3 4

Endpapers: A Tibetan lotus, the traditional
Buddhist symbol of enlightenment (see page 16).

· CONTENTS ·

WHO·ARE ·THE· BUDDHISTS?

Buddhists are people who follow the teachings of the son of an Indian nobleman, Siddhartha Gautama, who became known as the Buddha. He lived in India nearly 2,500 years ago. Buddhists use his teachings as a guide for their lives and as a way of understanding the world around them. They call their beliefs *Dharma* or *Buddha-Dharma*, the truth or teaching of the Buddha. Among the first Buddhists were monks who traveled widely through India and beyond, spreading the Buddha's message far and wide. Their teachings on truth, compassion and care for others soon gained them many followers.

EYES OF THE BUDDHA
This is the *stupa* of Bodhnath in Kathmandu, Nepal, one of the largest *stupas* in the world. A *stupa* is a sacred place for Buddhists, often built to house holy relics (see page 24) or texts, or to mark a special place in Buddhist history. The all-seeing eyes of the Buddha are painted on the four sides of the spire above the dome, keeping watch over the world below. The spire itself has 13 steps, one for each of the 13 stages on the journey to *nirvana* (see page 12). Legend says that one of the Buddha's bones is buried beneath the *stupa*, but no one knows for sure.

BUDDHIST MONKS
Some devout Buddhists give up their worldly goods and possessions and become monks and nuns. They spend their lives studying and chanting the sacred texts, learning to meditate and teaching. The first Buddhist monks included the Buddha's own son, Rahula, and his cousin, Ananda. They traveled around India, spreading the Buddha's message. In some Buddhist countries, such as Thailand and Myanmar (Burma), young boys spend time in a monastery as part of their education. Some of them go on to become monks. Others return home to their parents. The young monks in this picture come from Thailand. They are wearing traditional orange robes.

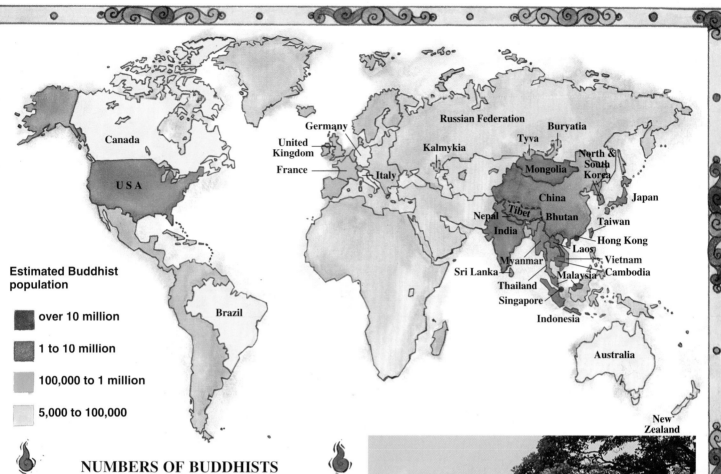

Estimated Buddhist population

- over 10 million
- 1 to 10 million
- 100,000 to 1 million
- 5,000 to 100,000

NUMBERS OF BUDDHISTS

There are probably about 400 million Buddhists in the world today, although it is hard to get an accurate total. The population of some countries is mostly Buddhist, but in other countries Buddhists are a minority. For example, about 92% of Thailand's 55 million people is Buddhist. Of Japan's 124 million people, 33% is Buddhist, but the 1,000,000 or so American Buddhists are 0.003% (1 in 3,000) of the population of the United States.

THE BUDDHIST WORLD

Some time after the Buddha's death, his followers split into two different groups, or schools. The Mahayana School, or 'Great Vehicle', spread to China, Vietnam, Korea, Japan, Nepal, Tibet and Mongolia. The Theravada School, or 'Way of the Elders', spread to Sri Lanka, Myanmar, Thailand and other parts of South-East Asia. Today, the majority of Buddhists still live in Asia where Buddhism began. More recently, in the early 20th century, Buddhism also spread to Europe and the USA. There are now many thousands of Buddhists in the West and lots of Buddhist temples and monasteries. This Peace Pagoda was built by Japanese Buddhists in London in 1985.

TIMELINE

THE DEVELOPMENT OF BUDDHISM

BCE = Before the Common Era = BC (term used by Christians)
CE = In the time of the Common Era = AD

c. 500BCE	c. 480BCE	c. 445BCE	c. 400BCE	400–314BCE
The Jain religion is founded in India by Mahavira. It spreads through west India but not beyond.	Siddhartha Gautama, the son of a nobleman, is born at Lumbini, Nepal. At the age of 29, he leaves his father's palace to begin his search for the meaning of life.	After meditating under a *bodhi* tree in Bodh Gaya, India, Gautama gains enlightenment and becomes the Buddha.	The death of the Buddha, aged 80, at Kushinagara, India. His followers travel far and wide, spreading his teachings through Asia.	Two councils are held to collect the Buddha's teachings together. After the second, different ways of practicing and interpreting Buddhism develop, including the Theravada school.

Siddhartha Gautama, the Buddha

CE1197	CE1191	12th Century CE	CE630–645	c. CE642
The great Buddhist University of Nalanda in India is destroyed by the Muslims. In its heyday in the seventh century CE, it had some 8,500 students and 1,500 teachers.	Zen Buddhism is introduced into Japan from China by the teacher and monk, Eisai.	Buddhism almost disappears from India. Hinduism and Islam are the major religions.	The Chinese Buddhist monk, Hsuan Tsang, visits Buddhist sites in India and worships the Buddha's relics. On his return to China he spends the rest of his life translating hundreds of Buddhist texts	Buddhism spreads to Tibet. The beautiful Jokhang Temple is built in Lhasa.

Buddha Shakyamuni, Jokhang Temple

CE1642

The fifth Dalai Lama becomes the religious and political leader of Tibet.

The Potala Palace, Lhasa

CE1643	CE1881	CE1891	CE1907	CE1930
The Potala Palace is built in Lhasa as the Dalai Lama's winter residence.	The Pali Text Society is founded for the translation and publication of Pali Buddhist texts into European languages.	The Mahabodhi Society is founded in Sri Lanka to unite Buddhists from all over the world and to raise funds for restoring the sacred Buddhist sites in India.	The first Buddhist Society in Britain is founded. This is followed by similar groups in France and Germany.	The Buddhist Society of America is formed.

EMPEROR ASHOKA

When Ashoka Maurya came to the throne in 268BCE, the Mauryan Empire was at the height of its power. In 259BCE, Ashoka launched a ferocious campaign against Kalinga on the east coast, and one of the few places to resist his rule. The campaign was successful, but in the bloody battle that followed 100,000 people were killed and thousands more wounded. Ashoka was filled with remorse. In an effort to make amends, he converted to Buddhism and vowed to practice its ideals of compassion and non-violence. Ashoka traveled widely through his empire, setting up pillars in places sacred to Buddhism. The pillars were inscribed with accounts of Ashoka's conversion and his thoughts on the *dharma*.

The wheel, symbol of Ashoka's kingship, now appears on the flag of India

BUDDHISM IN EXILE

From 1642 until 1951 in Tibet, the Dalai Lamas were the heads of government and the religious leaders of its Buddhist people. In 1951, however, the Chinese army invaded eastern Tibet and, in 1959, the present Dalai Lama was forced to flee. In 1965, Tibet was declared a province of China. Since then, hundreds of Buddhist monasteries have been destroyed, precious texts, paintings and statues burned, and thousands of monks arrested and killed. Thousands more monks have followed the Dalai Lama into exile in Dharamshala, India. From here, the Dalai Lama has campaigned long and hard for a free Tibet. But he has not yet been allowed to return to Lhasa, the capital of Tibet.

268–239BCE	c. 250BCE	80BCE
Reign of Emperor Ashoka Maurya, the greatest ruler of ancient India. Ashoka converts to Buddhism after seeing thousands of people killed in battle.	Ashoka's son and daughter are sent to Sri Lanka to spread the Buddha's teachings. Ashoka also sends missionaries to Burma and Thailand.	The Pali Canon, the main scripture of the Theravada Buddhists, is written down for the first time in Sri Lanka. Before this, the scriptures were passed down by monks through chanting.

Lion-headed top from a pillar of Ashoka

First Centuries BCE and CE

Mahayana Buddhism begins to develop. Buddhism spreads to China in the first century CE.

c. CE538	c. CE372	Second Century CE
Buddhism spreads to Japan. Between 1860 and 1945 it is replaced by Shinto as the official religion of Japan.	Buddhism spreads to Korea.	The first images are made of the Buddha. Before this, the Buddha was shown by symbols. Ashvaghosa, the Indian poet, writes one of the earliest biographies of the Buddha, called *Acts of the Buddha*.

Tenzin Gyatso the 14th Dalai Lama

CE1935	CE1967	CE1989
Birth of Tenzin Gyatso, the 14th and present Dalai Lama, the leader of Tibetan Buddhists.	The Friends of the Western Buddhist Order is started by an English monk, Sangharakshita. He wants to form a movement suited to the West and which combines parts of the Theravada, Tibetan and Zen traditions.	The Dalai Lama is awarded the Nobel Peace Prize in 1989. He continues to tour the world campaigning for peace, and for freedom for his country.

HOW·DID BUDDHISM ·BEGIN?·

Buddhism began with the teachings of a man called Siddhartha Gautama who lived in India about 2,500 years ago. Gautama was the son of a nobleman and was raised in great splendor in a palace. At the time of his birth, a wise man predicted that Gautama would become either a great ruler or a great holy man, depending on what he saw of life. Determined that this son should rule after him, his father shielded him from the influences of the outside world and did everything he could to make him happy. Gautama married his cousin, the beautiful princess Yashodara, and had a son, Rahula.

THE FOUR SIGHTS

Despite his life of luxury, Gautama felt trapped and unhappy. One day, against his father's wishes, he went riding in his chariot outside the palace walls. First, he saw an old man, then a sick man, racked with pain, then he saw the body of a dead man. Gautama was shocked by all this suffering. He asked his charioteer what it meant and was told that old age, sickness and death come to everyone eventually. Finally, he saw a holy man, dressed in simple robes. He seemed happy and contented. Gautama vowed to be like him and to search for the answer to the unhappiness he saw in the world. Can you see the four sights in the picture above?

USEFUL WORDS

Buddha	The 'enlightened' or 'awakened one'. The word used to describe Siddhartha Gautama. Buddhists believe that he is one of many *buddhas*, past and present.
Dharma	The teachings of the Buddha and the practice of them.
Sangha	Sometimes means Buddhist monks and nuns, and sometimes the whole Buddhist community.
Nirvana	The state of perfect bliss and happiness reached by those who have achieved enlightenment.
Enlightenment	Achieving enlightenment is like waking from a dream and seeing things as they really are and the truth behind everything.

GOING WITHOUT

One night, Gautama left the palace and dressed in monk's robes. For six years, he lived in the forest with five holy teachers. It was a very hard life. Gautama starved himself until he looked like a skeleton. But he did not find the answers he sought.

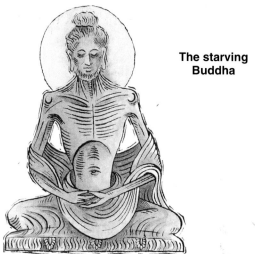

The starving Buddha

BECOMING THE BUDDHA

In desperation, Gautama left the forest and his companions behind, and made his way to the town of Bodh Gaya. Sitting under a great *bodhi* tree, he gained enlightenment, and spent the next 49 days and 49 nights meditating. He realized that people suffered because they were never content with what they had. They always wanted more. He also saw a way out of this unhappiness. From that time on, Gautama was known as the Buddha, the 'enlightened' or 'awakened one'.

LIFE AND DEATH

For the next 45 years, the Buddha traveled round India with a band of followers, living as a monk and teaching people how to overcome unhappiness. He died, aged 80, in the town of Kushinagara. This statue shows the Buddha lying on his side because this is how he died. Buddhists describe his death as *parinirvana*. It meant that his work as a *buddha* was done and he could enter *nirvana* for the final time. Legend says that an earthquake shook the earth when he first gained enlightenment and when he died.

·WHAT·DID· THE·BUDDHA ·TEACH?·

The Buddha knew from his own experience that happiness does not come from great luxury nor from great hardship. He taught people to follow a Middle Path between those two extremes. By following this path, people could overcome greed and desire, and the unhappiness they caused, and lead wiser, more caring lives in their quest to achieve enlightenment. The Buddha also taught that it was up to each individual to realize the truth for him or herself. His teachings were only meant as a guide to help them.

THE WHEEL OF LIFE
The painting on the left comes from Tibet. It shows Yama, Lord of Death, holding up the Wheel of Life – a very important symbol for Buddhists. It represents the cycle of birth, death and rebirth which is always turning like a wheel. Around the outside of the wheel, you can see the different stages of a person's life. Inside are different ways in which you might be reborn. The three animals in the center stand for hatred, greed and confusion. These stand in the way of a person's enlightenment.

 THE NOBLE EIGHTFOLD PATH

The Middle Path is also called the Noble Eightfold Path. The eight spokes of the *dharma*-wheel below represent the eight steps of the path. These steps are not separate, but they work together:

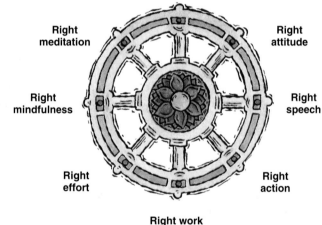

Right understanding

Right meditation

Right mindfulness

Right effort

Right work

Right attitude

Right speech

Right action

1. **Right understanding** – of the Buddha's teachings.

2. **Right attitude** – thinking kind thoughts.

3. **Right speech** – not telling lies or using angry words.

4. **Right action** – not harming any person or animal.

5. **Right work** – which does not make others suffer.

6. **Right effort** – thinking before you act.

7. **Right mindfulness** – being alert and aware.

8. **Right meditation** – for a calm, focused mind.

THE FOUR NOBLE TRUTHS

The Four Noble Truths form the most important part of the Buddha's teachings. They are:

1. **Life is full of unhappiness.**

2. **Unhappiness is caused by greed.**

3. **There is a way to end unhappiness.**

4. **The way to end unhappiness is the Middle Path.**

TEACHING TODAY

The Buddha spent the rest of his life as a monk, traveling around India, teaching the *dharma*. He also sent his followers out to spread his message. After his death, his followers continued his teaching. Teaching and studying the *dharma* is still an important part of Buddhism today. These Sri Lankan boys spend time in a monastery as part of their education. They learn about the Buddha and study ordinary school subjects. Some may stay on and become monks. Others leave when their education is complete.

THE BUDDHA'S TEACHING

After his enlightenment, the Buddha traveled to Sarnath where he gave his first talk in a park. To explain his teaching, he drew a wheel on the ground. This showed the endless round of life, death and rebirth in which everyone is caught up. To achieve enlightenment and escape from the cycle, he taught that people should follow the Middle Path. The picture above shows the Buddha teaching in the country-side. The five holy men he lived with in the forest became his first followers. But the number quickly grew as people heard the Buddha's words and asked to join him.

· W H A T · ELSE · DO · BUDDHISTS · BELIEVE ?

Buddhists believe that it is up to each person to take responsibility for his or her own actions and to realize the truth for themselves. If they act wisely and well, in accordance with the Buddha's teachings, they can live happier and more fulfilled lives. You do not need to be a special person to achieve this. Everyone has the potential to change his or her behavior for the better. Buddhists believe in the power of *karma,* which means that good actions lead to being reborn closer to *nirvana* and bad actions lead to being reborn further away from *nirvana.* Buddhists consider it fortunate to be born as a human being. They see it as an opportunity for developing good qualities such as compassion, patience, loving kindness, calmness and generosity. These are all things that will help them and other people to achieve true happiness.

THE THREE JEWELS

The three wheels in the picture on the right represent the Three Jewels of Buddhism. These are the Buddha himself, the *dharma,* or the Buddha's teaching, and the *sangha,* or Buddhist community. Buddhists take the Three Jewels as their guides through life and commit themselves to them (see page 38). They are called 'jewels' because they are so precious. Buddhists often describe the Buddha as a doctor, the *dharma* as a medicine and the *sangha* as the nurse who gives the medicine to a sick patient.

Lotus flowers

LOTUS FLOWERS

For Buddhists, lotus flowers are symbols of goodness and purity. Lotuses grow in water. But their flowers rise above the mud to bloom on the surface of the water. In the same way, people can rise above the trials and tribulations of life and achieve enlightenment. The lotus's beauty can also be compared to the Buddha.

THE THREE FIRES

Buddhists try to live a selfless life, in order to escape from the cycle of death and rebirth by reaching *nirvana.* To explain this, they use the story of a house burning with three fires of hatred, greed and ignorance which make people unhappy. Chanting, meditating and being kind to others all help to reduce the fires. When all three fires are put out, and unhappiness ends, there is *nirvana.*

BELONGING TO THE SANGHA

The *sangha*, or Buddhist community, is made up of monks, nuns and ordinary people. Belonging to the *sangha* is very important for Buddhists. By looking out for other people, it helps them to put aside any feelings of greed and selfishness, and to learn to share whatever they have with others. Helping other people is a central part of Buddhist life. These monks in Bhutan are blessing a gathering of worshipers. One way in which Buddhist monks help other people is to pass on the teachings of the Buddha and to help to lead them towards enlightenment. In some places, they may also offer people advice and help them if they have problems in their everyday lives.

CARING FOR THE EARTH

The monks in this picture come from the Samye Ling Tibetan Center in Scotland. In 1991, the Center launched the 'Holy Island Project', with the aim of turning Holy Island, off the Isle of Arran, into a retreat where people could go to meditate. It will also be a nature reserve. The community aims to be totally self-sufficient, getting all the food and water it needs from the island. Buddhists believe that it is vitally important to look after the earth and everything on it and to stop the destruction and pollution of the environment.

· D O E S · BUDDHISM · HAVE · ANY · GODS ?

Buddhists do not believe in an all-powerful God who created the world and watches over it. Neither is the Buddha worshiped as a god, but as a human being who gained enlightenment. Through his teaching and example, other human beings have the opportunity to achieve enlightenment for themselves. The Mahayana Buddhists (see page 20) also worship *bodhisattvas*. These are perfect, god-like figures who have gained enlightenment and so could now enter *nirvana*. Instead, they choose to be reborn and to stay in the world to help other people overcome their problems and gain enlightenment.

AVALOKITESHVARA

There are thousands of *bodhisattvas*. This painting shows Avalokiteshvara who is worshiped in Tibet for his great compassion and care for those who are unhappy. In the picture you can see his thousand arms in which he holds sacred symbols, such as a lotus and a wheel. Each hand also has an eye, which shows how Avalokiteshvara's help and compassion reach out to everyone at once. He is ready to help anyone in any kind of trouble. Around him are important figures from Tibetan Buddhism.

 CROSSING A RIVER

The Buddha did not want to be worshiped as a god or for people to accept things just because he said them. They should test his teachings or use them like a raft to cross a river. But they should not cling to them or be angry with them if they are criticized.

TARA

This modern painting shows the *bodhisattva* Green Tara, sitting in a lotus flower. Legend says that Tara was born from a lotus that sprouted from Avalokiteshvara's tears. Her task was to help him guide people towards enlightenment. You can see one of Tara's feet pointing towards the ground. This shows her willingness to help people overcome their unhappiness. Like Avalokiteshvara, Tara is worshiped for her great compassion.

GOLDEN BUDDHAS

In Buddhist temples and shrines, images of the Buddha and *bodhisattvas* remind people that they too can gain enlightenment, and they help them to think about the Buddha's teaching. This row of 394 golden statues of the Buddha stands in a temple called Wat Po in Thailand. (*Wat* is the Thai word for temple.) Buddhists believe that Siddhartha Gautama is one of many *buddhas*, past and future, who have gained enlightenment and *nirvana*,

THE BUDDHA TO COME

The next *buddha* will be Maitreya, shown on the right. At present he lives in one of the many Buddhist heavens, but he sometimes appears on earth to teach people. It is thought that his time will be a golden age when life will be better and enlightenment easier to achieve. This is a Japanese statue of Maitreya. In Japan, he is known as Miroku.

Maitreya

·ARE·THERE· DIFFERENT ·GROUPS·OF· BUDDHISTS?

As Buddhism moved out of India, after the Buddha's death, different groups began to appear. These spread to different countries and mixed with local beliefs and customs. All Buddhists share the same basic belief in the Three Jewels, (see page 16) but they have different ways of understanding the Buddha's teachings and of practicing their faith. The two main groups of Buddhism are the Theravada and Mahayana schools. Theravada Buddhists use the teachings of Gautama and say it is the Buddha alone who helps them through his message and example. Mahayana Buddhists also believe in 'heavenly' *buddhas* and *bodhisattvas,* who teach people and listen to their prayers. At the beginning of the 20th century, Buddhist groups also spread to Europe and America.

ZEN

Another type of Mahayana Buddhism, called Zen, is also practiced mainly in China and Japan. The word 'Zen' means 'meditation'. The aim of Zen Buddhists is to achieve enlightenment through meditation. Learning to meditate takes many years, but Zen Buddhists have developed many ways to help them, including writing poetry, painting and even practicing martial arts, such as karate and kung fu. These all help to focus the mind, even martial arts, because they teach you greater concentration and self-awareness. Zen paintings are very simple. The picture below shows a meditating frog, admired for its qualities of stillness and watchfulness.

A Zen painting

PURE LAND

Pure Land Buddhism is a type of Mahayana Buddhism. Its followers worship Amitabha, the *buddha* of infinite light, shown above. Amitabha is lord of a world known as a Pure Land, a beautiful, peaceful place. By praying to him and reciting his name, his followers believe they will go to the Pure Land when they die, and move closer to *nirvana.* Pure Land Buddhism is popular in China and Japan.

ZEN RIDDLES

Riddles, called *koans*, play an important part in Zen meditation. The master asks a riddle, such as, 'What is the sound of one hand clapping?' At first, the riddle does not seem to make sense. What is the answer? But the answer is not important. The aim of the riddle is to wake up your mind and teach it new ways of understanding.

TIBETAN BUDDHISM

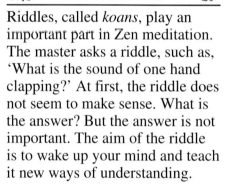

This is Sera monastery, one of the greatest Buddhist monasteries in Tibet. It was built in CE1419 by a monk called Tsong Khapa. In its heyday, the monastery was a great center of learning and meditation, and home to 5,000 monks. Fewer than 100 remain today. The main temple has many precious statues, *thangkas* (see page 41) and sacred books, but many more were destroyed when the Chinese invaded Tibet. Tibetan Buddhism is based on Mahayana teachings, but with many colorful rites and rituals. Buddhism came to Tibet from India in the seventh century CE.

MONKS AND GARDENS

The Zen monks above undergo very strict training. They work, study the scriptures, chant and meditate. They also go on pilgrimages to sacred sites. Here the monks are dressed in their traveling clothes – black robes, wicker hats, straw sandals and white trousers. An important part of many Zen monasteries is a sand garden, like the one above. Its simple design gives a feeling of peace and calmness and helps the monks in meditation.

· HOW · DO · BUDDHISTS · LIVE ? ·

Buddhists try to live their lives according to the Buddha's teachings. They remember that the Buddha said, 'Not to do any evil, to cultivate the good, to purify one's mind.' This involves making five promises, called Precepts (see opposite). It is not enough simply to make these promises. Buddhists try to follow them in everything they do. The Buddha taught people not to follow what he said blindly. People must think and test things out for themselves. Before you can help other people, you need to have a better understanding of yourself.

MEDITATION

Meditation is very important for Buddhists. They believe that training their minds will help them understand and 'rise above' ordinary thoughts and bring them closer to enlightenment. Most Buddhists meditate every day, on their own or in a group. They sit cross-legged on the floor, as this Western Buddhist is doing, eyes closed, concentrating on breathing calmly and regularly. Learning to meditate takes a lot of practice. It is not easy to empty your mind of all the thoughts buzzing around inside it. Some Buddhists concentrate on an object, such as a flower or a candle. Others chant to help them meditate. A popular chant is *Namo tassa bhagavato, arahato, sammaa-sambuddhassa*, which means 'Honor to the Lord, the saint, the perfectly and completely Enlightened One!' This is repeated three times and then followed by other chants, such as the Three Jewels and Five Precepts.

TELLING THE ROSARY

Some Buddhists count the beads of a *mala*, or rosary, as they meditate or chant. This *mala* has 108 beads, a sacred number. As he or she counts off the beads, the worshiper chants a *mantra*, or the name of the Buddha or a *bodhisattva*. This helps the worshiper to concentrate. The beads can also be used to count the number of chants being said.

THE FIVE PRECEPTS

In their everyday lives, Buddhists follow a set of guidelines called the Five Precepts or Promises.

1. **Not to harm or kill any living thing.** Because of this, some Buddhists choose to be vegetarians.

2. **Not to steal or take anything that is not freely given.**

3. **To control sexual desire.**

4. **Not to tell lies.**

5. **Not to drink or take drugs.**

A mandala

MANDALAS

A *mandala* is a circular picture used by Tibetan Buddhists to help them focus their attention as they meditate. Each part of the *mandala* has a special meaning. In the center is a figure or shape which symbolizes a particular quality, such as wisdom or compassion. This is sometimes a picture of a *bodhisattva*. Around this are four openings. These are the doorways you can go through to reach the quality in the center. Different colors also represent different qualities. Red stands for the Buddha's warmth and compassion, blue for his truth and teaching and white for his purity.

TEMPLE WORSHIP

When they visit the temple, Buddhists show their love and respect for the Buddha by bowing in front of his image, reciting the Three Jewels and making offerings. This woman is burning incense sticks in front of a huge statue of the Buddha. The sweet smell of incense reminds the worshiper of the beauty of the Buddha's teachings. As the offering is made, the worshiper may say a chant like the one below:

*'Him of fragrant face and body,
Fragrant with infinite virtues,
I honor the Truth-knowing One
with fragrant incense.'*

You can read more about how Buddhists worship on pages 26–7.

·WHERE·DO· BUDDHISTS ·WORSHIP?·

Buddhists often worship on their own at home, or join other Buddhists to worship and meditate in a group. Many visit temples and monasteries to chant, make offerings and listen to talks given by the monks. At home or in the temple, they worship in front of a shrine containing an image of the Buddha or of a *bodhisattva*, surrounded by incense, candles and flowers. The very first Buddhist shrines were called *stupas*. When the Buddha died, his body was cremated and his ashes taken to eight different places, where *stupas* were built over them. Emperor Ashoka later redivided the ashes called 'relics' and put them in new *stupas* all over India. Other *stupas* hold relics of important monks and sacred texts.

A SHRINE AT HOME

A shrine may be part of a temple or monastery, or it may be a room or a part of a room in an ordinary house. Here the family can offer flowers, candles and incense to an image of the Buddha. This small shrine is in a house in Sri Lanka. There are several statues of the Buddha, a lamp and a packet of incense sticks. Every day members of the family stand in front of the shrine and recite the Three Jewels and the Five Precepts to renew their commitment to the Buddha, the *dharma* and the *sangha*.

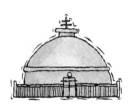 **STYLES OF STUPA**

The first *stupas* were shaped like domes. But as Buddhism spread to different countries, different styles developed. In China and Japan, *stupas* became tall, thin *pagodas*. Their shape represents the five elements of the universe – earth, water, fire, wind and space.

1. Stupa (India)   **2. Dagoba (Sri Lanka)**   **3. Chorten (Tibet)**   **4. Pagoda (China/Japan)**

THE JOKHANG TEMPLE

Trays of yak-butter lamps burn brightly inside the Jokhang Temple in Lhasa, Tibet. At least one lamp is kept burning all the time. As part of their worship, Buddhists place candles or lamps in front of the statue of the Buddha or *bodhisattva* in the shrine. The light that shines out is seen as a symbol of the enlightenment that the Buddha's teaching brings. The Jokhang is the most important temple in Tibet. Legend says that it was built in about CE650, on the site of a magical underground lake in which people could see the future.

SHWEDAGON

This is part of the beautiful Shwedagon Pagoda complex in Myanmar. The *pagoda* is said to contain eight of the Buddha's hairs and is one of the most sacred Buddhist sites. The gleaming towers are covered in gold, gifts from Buddhists who hope to gain good *karma* to help them in their next lives. The top of the main *pagoda* is encrusted with rubies and diamonds, capped with a huge emerald.

PRAYER FLAGS

In Tibet, prayer flags like these flutter from every temple and monastery. The prayers printed on them are blown by the wind all over the world.

Prayer flags

· H O W · D O · BUDDHISTS · WORSHIP ? ·

When Buddhists visit the temple, they put their hands together in greeting, then kneel and bow three times before the statue of the Buddha or *bodhisattva* in the shrine-room. The three bows are to represent the Buddha, the *dharma* and the *sangha*. Then they offer gifts of flowers, candles, incense and food. The gifts show their respect for the Buddha and their thanks for his teaching. They repeat the Five Precepts and pledge their commitment to the Three Jewels. They may also spend some time meditating, chanting or listening to monks reading from the sacred texts. Buddhists visit the temple whenever they wish, but especially on full moon days and some festivals.

INSIDE THE TEMPLE

These Buddhists are worshiping in the main shrine-room of the Shwedagon Pagoda in Burma. They have taken off their shoes as a mark of respect. The shrine is beautifully decorated, with several golden statues of the Buddha. These statues remind people of the Buddha's good qualities and teaching, and of the possibility of gaining enlightenment by following his example.

TEMPLE OFFERINGS

Worshipers take offerings of candles, flowers and incense to place on the shrine in front of the Buddha. Candles are lit to represent the light offered by the Buddha's teachings which help to get rid of the darkness of ignorance. Flowers look and smell sweet but they wilt and die, a reminder of the teaching that nothing lasts for ever. People chant or say prayers as they make their offerings. They may also leave gifts of food for the monks. Making offerings is believed to be a way of gaining good *karma* and of moving closer to *nirvana*.

🏵 A BUDDHIST CHANT 🏵

This is a Buddhist chant from the *Metta Sutta* which encourages kindness and compassion to others:

May all beings be happy,
Whatever they are,
Weak or strong,
Tall, short or medium,
Small or large.
May all without exception
be happy,
Beings seen or unseen,
Those who live near or far away,
Those who are born
And those who are yet to be born.
May all beings be happy.

Prayer wheel

PRAYER WHEELS

As she walks around the temple, this Tibetan woman tells her rosary in one hand and spins the huge prayer wheels with the other. A prayer wheel is a cylinder with a paper scroll inside. Thousands of prayers are written on the scroll. By spinning the wheels, she releases the prayers into the world. Worshipers always walk around holy places in a clockwise direction, spinning the wheels with their right hands. This is because they believe that they should move around the Buddha in the same way as the planets move around the sun. They also repeat the sacred mantra, *Om mani padme hum*, or 'Praise to the jewel in the lotus'.

TIBETAN WORSHIP

The objects shown here are also used as part of Tibetan worship. Above is a hand-held prayer wheel, which people can spin as they walk. The bell on the right represents wisdom. It is rung during religious ceremonies. The unusual object next to it is called a *vajra*. It is the symbol of the Buddha's power and of the truth behind everything.

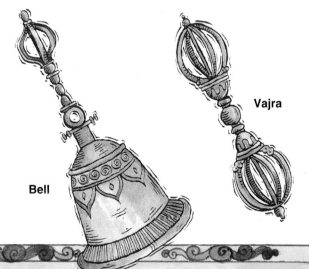

Bell

Vajra

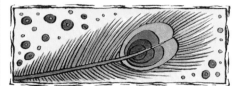

WHO ARE THE BUDDHIST HOLY MEN AND WOMEN?

Some devout Buddhists leave their homes and possessions and dedicate their lives to practicing, studying and preaching the Buddha's message. They are the monastic *sangha*, or community, of Buddhist monks called *bhikkhus*, and nuns. Among the first Buddhist monks were the five holy men who lived in the forest with the Buddha (see page 13), together with his son, Rahula, and his cousin, Ananda. After his enlightenment, the Buddha himself lived the life of a wandering monk, traveling through India with his fellow *bhikkhus*, teaching the *dharma*. The monks relied on gifts of food to sustain them and spent the rainy season in *viharas*, or monasteries, built by wealthy followers. The first *viharas* were simple huts.

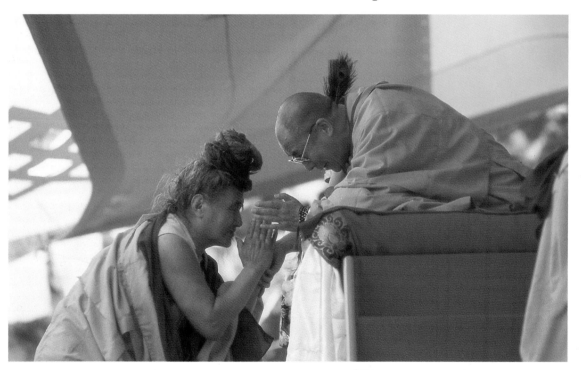

THE DALAI LAMA

In Tibetan Buddhism, respected teachers are known as *lamas*. The Dalai Lama, shown above, is the leader of Tibet's Buddhists. His title means 'a teacher whose wisdom is as deep as the ocean'. Tibetans believe that the Dalai Lama is the *bodhisattva*, Avalokiteshvara, in human form. When one Dalai Lama dies, Avalokiteshvara's spirit is reborn in the body of another baby boy. A long search begins to find the child. Then he is taken to Lhasa, the capital of Tibet, to be trained in his sacred duties.

FIRST MONKS

This is what the Buddha said to his first monks when he sent them out to teach the *dharma*:

'Go forth, O monks, for the joy and well-being of many, out of compassion for the world.
Go not two together on the same path.
Preach, O monks, the message which is noble in its beginning, in its course and in its end.
Proclaim the noble path.'

BUDDHIST NUNS

These women are being ordained as Buddhist nuns in Britain. At first, women were not allowed to join the *sangha*. But, an early text says, the Buddha was later persuaded by his disciple Ananda, at his step-mother's request, to admit women to the community. Like Buddhist monks, nuns live very simply and own very few personal belongings. In China nuns follow the same strict rules as the monks. In Tibet and Theravada countries, they follow Ten or Eight Precepts and have a lower status than monks.

GIVING ALMS

In Theravada countries, such as Thailand, monks rely on local people for their food. Every morning, they leave the monastery so that people can fill their alms bowls with rice, vegetables and fruit. The monks are not allowed to ask for food. But people are happy to give it to them. By giving gifts to the monks, they hope to gain good *karma* to help them on their path to *nirvana*. The monks take their food back to the monastery to share with the other monks.

Alms bowl

Khata

GIFT OF A SCARF

In Tibet, white scarves, called *khatas*, are offered as gifts and marks of respect to monks and *lamas* (religious teachers). They are used instead of flowers which are very scarce in Tibet. *Khata* are also draped around statues of the Buddha and *bodhisattvas*.

WHAT·IS·LIFE LIKE·IN·A BUDDHIST MONASTERY?

Monks and nuns lead simple, strict lives, studying the sacred texts, learning to chant and meditate, and helping in the daily running of the monastery. Some also work or teach in the local community. The monks and nuns obey a set of monastery rules called the *vinaya*. Many monasteries have 227 rules, but the number can vary. The rules include the Ten Precepts, which the monks vow to keep. These are the Five Precepts which ordinary Buddhists follow (see page 23), together with five extra rules – not eating after midday, not singing or dancing in a frivolous way, not wearing perfume or jewelry, not sleeping on a soft bed and not taking gifts of money.

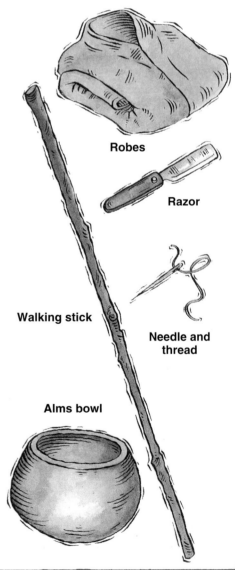

Robes

Razor

Walking stick

Needle and thread

Alms bowl

MONKS IN TIBET

These Tibetan monks are performing a special sacred dance, called *cham*, in the courtyard of their monastery. They are carrying offerings of white scarves and blowing long trumpets called *shawms*. Until the invasion by China, ceremonies like this were widespread in Tibet and were held to celebrate festivals and special occasions. These monks belong to the *Gelupka*, or Yellow Hat, group. Their name comes from the color of their ceremonial hats. The height of the crests on each hat shows how learned its wearer is. The Dalai Lama is the leader of the Yellow Hats.

DAILY MEAL

As part of their simple lifestyle, these monks in Thailand have only two meals a day. The first is eaten early in the morning, at about 7 a.m. The second must be eaten before noon. The meals are made up of the food placed in the monks' alms bowls that morning by the local people. After this the monks fast (do not eat) until the next morning, with only water or tea without milk or sugar to drink. This teaches them self-discipline and helps them to train their minds.

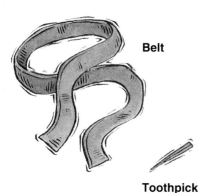

Belt

Toothpick

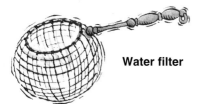

Water filter

THE EIGHT REQUISITES

Traditionally, monks are only allowed to own eight things. These are called the Eight Requisites.

1. **Robes (saffron, maroon or black)**
2. **A belt**
3. **An alms bowl**
4. **A needle and thread**
5. **A walking stick**
6. **A razor**
7. **A toothpick**
8. **A filter for straining water and removing any live creatures which might otherwise be swallowed.**

WORK AND STUDY

As part of his duties, this Tibetan monk is cleaning out the pots and pans. Monks help to care for, run and repair the monastery, as well as organizing ceremonies and festivals. But most of their time is spent studying the sacred texts, chanting and meditating. The three biggest Tibetan monasteries, Drepung, Sera and Ganden, award a special degree to monks who have studied for at least 20 years and achieved a very high standard of knowledge. Boys can enter a monastery at any age but they do not take their vows and become fully ordained until the age of 20.

· WHICH · ARE · THE · BUDDHIST · SACRED · TEXTS ? ·

Until the first century BCE, the Buddha's teachings were passed down from one generation to the next by word of mouth. Then, about 320 years after his death, they were finally written down in the ancient language of Pali. These writings were called the Pali Canon and became the sacred texts of the Theravada Buddhists. Mahayana Buddhists have their own set of scriptures, and many are called *sutras*. These use parables and stories to explain difficult parts of the Buddha's teaching and to talk about his life. Other Buddhist texts include those based on the works of great Buddhist teachers and monks, such as Milarepa, a key figure in Tibetan Buddhism.

A MONASTERY LIBRARY
These Tibetan monks are busy making books in the monastery library. The first Buddhist texts were written down on palm leaves. The rectangular pages of these Tibetan books are a reminder of the long, narrow shape of the leaves. As Buddhism spread from India, the sacred texts had to be translated into different languages. Many monks traveled to India from China and Tibet in search of manuscripts. It was painstaking work and the monks who performed it were treated with great honor and respect. As you can see, translation and copying work continues in Tibet today.

THE DHAMMAPADA

These extracts come from the *Dhammapada*, a collection of the Buddha's sayings, which form part of the Pali Canon.

'If a man has faith and virtue, then he has true glory and treasure. Wherever that man may go, there he will be held in honor.'

'When a man has something to do, let him do it with all his might.'

'Better than a thousand useless words is one single word that brings peace.

Better than a thousand useless verses is one single verse that brings peace.

Better than a hundred useless poems is one single poem that brings peace.'

'Conquer anger by love; conquer evil by good; conquer the mean by giving; conquer the liar by truth.'

'A thoughtless pilgrim only raises dust on the road.'

THE THREE BASKETS

The Pali Canon is also called the *Tripitaka*, or Three Baskets. The first basket, or section, contains rules for monks and nuns to follow. The second contains the *dharma*, or teachings of the Buddha. The third basket contains writings that explain this teaching. Theravada Buddhists believe that the *Tripitaka* is the most accurate record of what the Buddha actually taught. Studying, chanting, discussing and learning the sacred texts is an important part of every Buddhist monk's life. These young monks are chanting from sacred texts.

BUDDHIST LANGUAGES

Some monks still read and recite the scriptures in the ancient Indian language of Pali, although translations are often used. The Mahayana texts were written in another ancient language, called Sanskrit. This is a passage from the *Dhammapada*:

Sabba-pāpassa akaranam,
kusalassa upasampadā
sa-citta-pariyodapanam
etam buddhāna sāsanam

Not to do any evil,
to cultivate the good,
to purify one's mind:
this is the teaching of the Buddhas.

DIAMOND SUTRA

This is a page from the *Diamond Sutra*, one of the most important Mahayana texts. It was originally written in the fourth century CE. This copy from the British Museum is from CE868, and is the oldest known book left in existence. The *Sutra* is about Buddhist philosophy. Another popular text is the *Lotus Sutra*. It explains the different teachings used by the Buddha to help people achieve enlightenment. Although there are many ways, it says, they all lead to the same goal. There are many other *sutras* besides these.

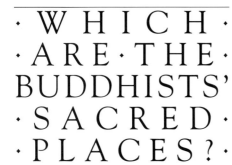

·WHICH· ·ARE·THE· BUDDHISTS' ·SACRED· ·PLACES?·

Many of the most sacred places of Buddhism are those connected with events in the Buddha's life. These include Lumbini in Nepal, where the Buddha was born, and three places in India – Bodh Gaya, where he achieved enlightenment, Sarnath, where he taught for the first time, and Kushinagara, where he died. Buddhist pilgrims – monks, nuns and ordinary people – come from all over the world to visit these holy sites and thousands of other temples, *stupas* and shrines across the Buddhist world. There are many reasons for making these special journeys, or pilgrimages. They help people to feel closer to the Buddha and his teaching, and to gain good *karma* which will help them get nearer to *nirvana*.

SACRED PLACES

This map shows some of the holiest places for Buddhists. They include places connected with the life of the Buddha himself and other sacred places mentioned throughout this book.

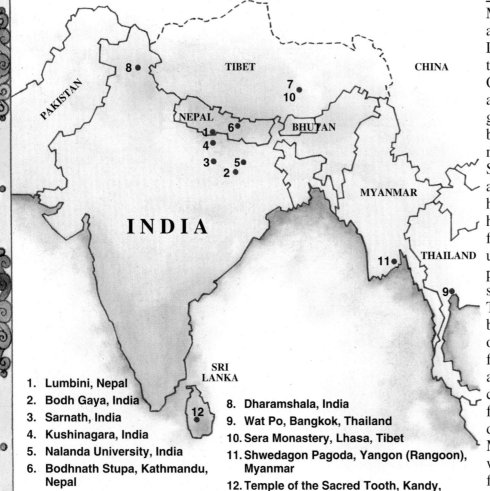

1. **Lumbini, Nepal**
2. **Bodh Gaya, India**
3. **Sarnath, India**
4. **Kushinagara, India**
5. **Nalanda University, India**
6. **Bodhnath Stupa, Kathmandu, Nepal**
7. **Jokhang Temple, Lhasa, Tibet**
8. **Dharamshala, India**
9. **Wat Po, Bangkok, Thailand**
10. **Sera Monastery, Lhasa, Tibet**
11. **Shwedagon Pagoda, Yangon (Rangoon), Myanmar**
12. **Temple of the Sacred Tooth, Kandy, Sri Lanka**

THE BUDDHA'S BIRTH

Many legends have been told about the birth of the Buddha in Lumbini, Nepal. The most famous tells how the Buddha's mother, Queen Maya, had a dream about a white elephant, the sign of great good fortune. The sign proved to be true. Some time later, on the night of the full moon in May, Siddhartha Gautama was born in a woodland grove in Lumbini, as his mother was on her way to visit her parents. As the baby was born, from his mother's side, many unusual and magical events took place. Legend says that the earth shook and was flooded with light. The trees in the grove burst into bloom and two streams of water, one hot, one cold, flowed down from the sky. Blind people were able to see again, lame people could walk and prisoners were freed from their chains. Seven days after her son's birth, Queen Maya died. The young Gautama was brought up by his aunt in his father's luxurious palace.

BODH GAYA

Each year, thousands of pilgrims flock to Bodh Gaya, the place where the Buddha achieved enlightenment. A *bodhi* tree still growing there is said to be descended from the very tree under which the Buddha sat to meditate. The picture below shows the famous Mahabodhi Temple, the focus of every pilgrim's journey to the town. The pilgrims come here to meditate and to leave offerings before the great golden statue of the Buddha inside.

SARNATH STUPA

Above is the Dhamekh Stupa in Sarnath, northern India. The *stupa* is believed to stand on the very spot where the Buddha preached his first sermon after his enlightenment. Pilgrims walk three times around the *stupa*, once for each of the Three Jewels (the Buddha, the *dharma* and the *sangha*). They always walk in a clockwise direction, keeping their right side towards the shrine (see page 27).

TIBETAN PILGRIMAGE

For Tibetan Buddhists, many of their most sacred places lie in and around Lhasa. Among them are temples, monasteries and the Dalai Lama's palaces. This pilgrim is standing in front of the Jokhang Temple, one of the holiest places of all. She is about to prostrate herself (lie full length) on the ground as part of her worship. This is called *kjangchag*. It is thought to be very holy, particularly in May, the month of the Buddha's birthday. Some pilgrims travel long distances to Lhasa at this time, prostrating themselves the whole way. When they reach Lhasa, they follow three special pilgrimage routes. One runs around the city. The second and third run around the outside and inside of the Jokhang Temple.

·WHAT·ARE· THE·MAIN BUDDHIST FESTIVALS?

There are many Buddhist festivals throughout the year. The most important mark events in the Buddha's life, such as his birth and enlightenment. Some are celebrated all around the Buddhist world. But the way they are celebrated varies from country to country, depending on local customs and traditions. Festivals are joyful times, when Buddhists visit the temple or monastery, taking offerings and gifts for the monks and nuns. The most important are celebrated on full moon days when it is thought the main events in the Buddha's life happened.

FESTIVAL OF THE SACRED TOOTH

Each year, on the night of the August full moon, a special festival is held in Kandy, Sri Lanka. A magnificent procession of elephants parades through the town. On its back, the largest elephant carries a miniature golden *stupa* which contains a very precious relic, a sacred tooth, said to have belonged to the Buddha himself. Huge, noisy crowds line the route, with fire-eaters, dancers and drummers. For the rest of the year, the sacred tooth is kept in a nearby temple.

 NEW ROBES

In the early days of Buddhism, the monks had to shelter in one place during the monsoon when heavy rains made it impossible to travel. They used this time, called the 'rains retreat', for meditation and study. In Thailand, a festival is held to mark the end of the rainy season in November. It is called Kathina. At a joyful ceremony, the local people go to the monastery and present the monks with gifts to thank them for all the work they do during the year. The most important gift is new robes.

WESAK

On the day of the full moon in May, Theravada Buddhists all over the world celebrate the festival of Wesak when they remember the Buddha's birth, enlightenment and death. It is the happiest day of the year. People visit the temple and decorate their houses with lanterns and flowers. There are lively processions through the streets and special ceremonies are held. These children are greeting their parents on the day of Wesak with a gift of flowers. They also send Wesak cards to their friends.

LOI KRATONG

Loi Kratong is the Thai festival of light, held on the night of the November full moon. As the moon rises, people gather by the river bank and place lamps, made of leaves and candles, on the water. As these float away, they are thought to carry bad luck with them. People also listen to the story of one of the Buddha's past lives as Prince Vessantara who was famous for his compassion and generosity.

Lamp floating on the river for Loi Kratong

HANA MATSURI

These Japanese children are dressed up to celebrate Hana Matsuri, an important Mahayana festival. It is held on April 8th, the day on which Japanese Buddhists celebrate the birth of the Buddha. The children are wearing flowers in their hair to honor the Buddha and because this festival also celebrates the coming of spring. They are lining up to visit the temple. Here they will pour scented tea over a statue of the baby Buddha. This reminds them of the Buddha's first bath when the gods poured two streams of scented water from the sky to wash him (see page 34).

·WHAT·ARE· THE·MOST IMPORTANT TIMES·IN·A BUDDHIST'S ·LIFE?·

The important times in a Buddhist's life are marked in different ways in different countries, according to local customs. The birth of a baby is a particularly happy time. In Theravada countries, although no set ceremonies have to be performed, monks are often invited into the home to chant passages from the sacred texts. When the baby is about a month old, it may be taken to the temple and given a name. Buddhist parents try to bring up their children according to the Buddha's teachings. Family life is very important. The Buddha compared a family to a group of trees in a forest, able to withstand the force of the wind because they support each other. A tree on its own is easily blown down.

BECOMING A BUDDHIST

Some people are born into Buddhist families. Others become Buddhists later or convert to Buddhism from another faith. To become a Buddhist, you make a commitment to the Three Jewels by reciting the following words: '*I go to the Buddha for refuge. I go to the* dharma *for refuge. I go to the* sangha *for refuge.*'

BUDDHIST WEDDINGS

In many Buddhist countries, people marry someone chosen by their family. The wedding takes place at the bride's home. A monk may be invited to the house to bless the couple and read from the scriptures. But he does not take part in the wedding ceremony itself. This may be conducted by an uncle or cousin. The couple stand on a special platform called a *purowa*. They may exchange rings and vows, and have their hands joined with a silk scarf to symbolize their marriage. After the ceremony, there is a special feast.

JOINING A MONASTERY

A young boy from Myanmar is being dressed in maroon robes, ready to be admitted into the monastery. He has also had his head shaved to show that he has turned away from worldly ties. He is about 10 years old. In countries such as Myanmar and Thailand, many young boys spend a short time in a monastery as part of their education. For a while, they live as junior monks and their ordination (joining) ceremony is one of the most important times in their lives. The robes and shaved head are signs that a monk has given up his attachment to the world and devoted his life to the teachings of the Buddha. In some countries such as Thailand, monks wear saffron (orange-yellow) robes. In others such as Myanmar and Tibet, their robes are maroon and in Japan they are black. During the ceremony, the boy must pledge his commitment to the Three Jewels and recite the Ten Precepts (see page 30).

WESTERN BUDDHISTS

Members of a group called Friends of the Western Buddhist Order do not wear robes to show their commitment. Instead they wear a white cloth band, called a *kesa* (see right), around their shoulders. It is embroidered with an emblem showing the Three Jewels. They also take a new name, such as Ananda (meaning joy), to mark the start of their new life.

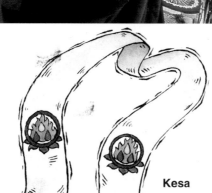

Kesa

FUNERAL

Buddhists believe that nothing lasts for ever. Everything is always changing. It is very sad when someone dies, but it is also a natural part of this process of change. If a person has led a good life, the next life may bring him or her closer to *nirvana*. When a Buddhist dies, he or she may be buried or cremated. Monks comfort the family and conduct the funeral ceremony. Friends and relatives of the dead person do good deeds on their behalf by giving food and other gifts to the monks, nuns and to the poor and needy.

·WHAT·IS· BUDDHIST ·ART·LIKE?·

The earliest works of Buddhist art were carvings and cave paintings that showed scenes from the Buddha's life. The Buddha himself was never shown in person. Symbols were used instead (see opposite). As Buddhism spread out of India, it inspired many styles of art. Statues of the Buddha and *bodhisattvas* began to be made for temples and monasteries in India and beyond, together with beautiful paintings and designs. But Buddhist art is not just decorative. The statues and symbols help to express deep feelings and beliefs that can be difficult to put into words.

IMAGE OF THE BUDDHA

Statues of the Buddha always show a variety of signs that mark him out as an extraordinary person. This modern statue shows the Buddha with long earlobes, a sign that he came from a noble family (which meant he had worn heavy earrings). He also has tightly curled hair, a sign that he was a very important man. His hands are in the *mudra*, or gesture, of concentration and meditation.

MUDRAS

The positions of the hands and fingers in statues of the Buddha and *bodhisattvas* have special meanings. These hand gestures are called *mudras*.

This *mudra* represents a wheel turning, which is how the Buddha explained his teaching.

This *mudra* shows one hand raised in a gesture of protection. The other hand shows compassion and the granting of a wish.

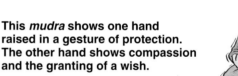

This *mudra* is described as 'calling the earth to witness'. Just before he became enlightened, the Buddha touched the earth with his hand so that, by shaking, it witnessed his past good deeds.

This is the *mudra* of teaching. One hand shows the shape of a wheel which represents the *dharma*. The other is the sign of reasoning.

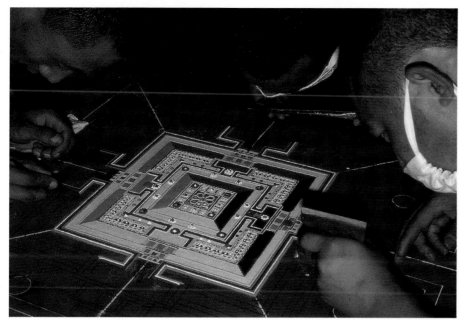

SAND MANDALA

These Tibetan monks are tracing out a complicated *mandala* in colored sand, ready for a festival or religious ceremony. (You can read about *mandalas* on page 23). It takes great skill, good eyesight and a steady hand. The monks wear masks to stop them blowing the sand out of position. Young monks spend many hours learning to make these sacred designs, starting with much simpler patterns. After the festival, the *mandala* will be destroyed and made again the following year. *Mandalas* are also made of yak butter and even of plastic!

THE BUDDHA'S FOOTPRINTS

The footprints on the right are one of the symbols used to show the Buddha's presence in the earliest types of Buddhist art. Other symbols used by the artists were a wheel, a *stupa*, a horse, a lotus flower, a *bodhi* tree and a royal umbrella held over an empty throne. Each of these symbols represented a particular part of the Buddha's life and teaching.

The Buddha's footprints

THANGKA CEREMONY

These monks are unfurling a huge *thangka* painting for a great open-air ceremony at the Sera Monastery in Tibet. A *thangka* is a sacred Buddhist painting, drawn on silk or cotton cloth so that it can be rolled up and carried about. Some *thangkas* show pictures of *bodhisattvas*, scenes from Buddhist history or symbols such as the Wheel of Life (see page 14). Ancient rules govern which shapes, colors and patterns artists can use. Tibetan Buddhists use *thangkas*, large and small, to help them meditate.

· D O · BUDDHISTS · L I K E · · S T O R I E S ?

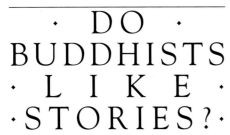

Buddhists tell stories to help them both explain and understand the *dharma*. Many of these stories were first told by the Buddha himself. A skilful teacher and storyteller, he often used stories and parables to get his message across. Stories were also told about the Buddha by his followers and these too have been passed down to the present day. Among the most popular Buddhist stories are the *Jatakas*, a collection of hundreds of tales about the Buddha's past lives. In many of these stories, the Buddha appears in animal form to teach the value of good qualities, such as compassion, wisdom, patience or generosity. The *Jatakas* are part of the Pali Canon. Buddhists use stories to teach children about Buddhism and to help them understand Buddhist teachings on sharing, helping others and the value of friendship.

 PAST LIVES

In many of the *Jatakas*, the Buddha is reborn as an animal. Here are just a few of his previous lives.

Golden peacock
The Buddha appeared as a beautiful peacock who was tricked into being caught, in a story to show that nobody is perfect.

Hare
The Buddha was born as a wise hare, in a story to show the merit of being kind and generous to people less well off than yourself.

Golden stag
In several stories, the Buddha appeared as a stag to show the virtue of making sacrifices in your own life in order to help others.

Lion
The Buddha often appeared as a lion, the king of the beasts, in stories to show the danger of trying to be something that you are not.

White elephant
In several past lives, the Buddha appeared as an elephant in stories to show the danger of acting badly towards others.

White horse
The Buddha was once born as a white horse in a story to show the importance of following the *dharma*.

THE STORY OF THE LION AND THE JACKAL

In this *Jataka* story, the Buddha shows that
one good turn deserves another.

In one of his past lives, the Buddha was born as a lion who lived on a high mountain. The foot of the mountain was surrounded by water, with just one small island of marshy land. On the island lived rabbits and deer.

One day the lion saw a deer grazing on the island below and bounded down towards it. But as he pounced, he sunk into the wet, marshy ground. His feet caught fast in the mud and for seven days he could not move or hunt for food.

On the seventh day, a jackal saw him and fled in terror. He thought the lion would eat him. But the lion called him back and asked him to help him. 'If you can set me free,' he said, 'I promise not to eat you.' So the jackal scooped the mud away and pushed and pulled until the lion was free.

By now the lion was very hungry indeed. He killed a bull and asked the jackal to share his feast. 'To thank you for saving me,' he said. At the end of their meal, the lion asked the jackal if he wanted to come and live with him. 'There's a small cave next to mine,' he told him. 'If you lived there, then I could look after you.'

So the jackal went home to fetch his wife and children, and they all went to live near the lion. For a while, all was well. The two families lived happily together and, with the lion to protect them, the jackals all felt safe. But, after some time, things began to change. The lioness felt jealous that her husband spent so much time with the jackal and his family. She even hinted to the jackal's wife that it was time for them to move on.

The jackal's wife told her husband and one day, when the lion and the jackal were out hunting together, the jackal told the lion they would soon be moving on. 'But why didn't you ask us to leave before if you felt like that?' he asked the lion. 'You are so strong and powerful, we would not have argued.'

The lion was amazed. He told the jackal he did not want him to leave at all. Where had he got this silly idea from? And so the truth came out.

When the lion reached home, he reminded his wife of the time he had been stuck in the mud, with nothing to eat for seven days, and how the jackal had freed him. 'However small and lowly he is,' he told his wife, 'that jackal saved my life. That makes him my friend, for ever.' And now the lioness understood. And once again, the lions and the jackals lived in peace and friendship. For one good turn deserves another.

·GLOSSARY·

ALMS Donations or gifts of food, money or robes, given to monks, nuns and to the poor.

BHIKKHU A Buddhist monk.

BODHISATTVA An enlightened person who chooses to be reborn and stay in the world to help other people gain enlightenment too.

BODHI TREE A sacred fig tree under which Gautama became the Buddha. 'Bodhi' means 'enlightenment'. Some people take the name 'Bodhi' when they become a Buddhist.

BUDDHA The title given to Siddhartha Gautama when he achieved enlightenment. It means 'enlightened one' or 'awakened one'.

CHANTING Half-singing, half-speaking a phrase or text. It is very calming and peaceful to do and to listen to.

COMPASSION Care and kindness towards others.

CREMATED When the body of dead person is burned to ashes rather than buried.

DHARMA The Buddha's teachings and practice of them.

ENLIGHTENMENT Like waking up from a deep sleep and being able to see the true meaning of life.

JATAKA A popular collection of stories about the Buddha's past lives.

KARMA Your actions, good or bad, and their results, good or bad. Good actions lead you closer to *nirvana*; bad actions lead further away.

KHATA A white scarf offered as a mark of respect in Tibet.

NIRVANA A state of perfect bliss and happiness reached by those who have become enlightened.

MANDALA A circular design or picture used by some Buddhists to help them meditate.

MANTRA A sacred word or phrase which is chanted during worship or meditation.

MARTIAL ARTS Traditional methods of self defense, such as karate and kung fu, originally used to train soldiers for war.

MEDITATION Sitting quietly and focusing your mind to achieve inner calm and peace.

MISSIONARIES People who travel from place to place teaching others about their faith and beliefs.

MONASTERY A place where monks or nuns live, worship and study.

MONSOON The rainy season in many tropical countries.

MUDRAS Hand gestures seen on statues of the Buddha and *bodhisattvas*. Each *mudra* has a special meaning.

ORDINATION The ceremony held when a person becomes a monk or nun, and joins a monastery.

PAGODA A style of *stupa* found in China and Japan.

PALI An ancient Indian language. The sacred books of the Theravada Buddhists were first written down in Pali.

PARABLE A kind of story used in many religions that helps to explain a difficult idea or message.

PILGRIMAGE A special journey to a holy place, such as a temple, shrine or a sacred mountain or river.

REBIRTH The belief that your innermost energies are reborn in a different body when you die.

RELIC Something which once belonged to a holy person, or even a part of the body.

RITUAL A religious ceremony.

ROSARY A string of beads that Buddhists use to help them chant and meditate.

SAFFRON The orange-yellow color of monks' robes in many Buddhist countries. Saffron is a holy color in India, where Buddhism began.

SANGHA The Buddhist community, including monks, nuns and, more generally, all Buddhists.

SANSKRIT An ancient Indian language. The sacred texts of the Mahayana Buddhists were written down in Sanskrit.

SCRIPTURES Sacred texts.

SHRINE An altar holding Buddhist images and used for worship. Found in temples and special places in homes.

STUPA A sacred structure which contains relics, texts or marks a special place in Buddhist history.

THANKGA A sacred Buddhist painting from Tibet.

VIHARA A Buddhist monastery.

VINAYA A set of 227 or more rules for monks and nuns that helps them to calm their minds and control greed.

· I N D E X ·